J 948.022 HUE
Huey, Lois Miner.
American archaeology
uncovers the Vikings /

D1377675

PALM BEACH COUNTY
LIBRARY SYSTEM
3650 SUMMIT BLVD.
WEST PALM BEACH, FLORIDA 33406

American Archaeology

UNCOVERS

THE VIKINGS

LOIS MINER HUEY

Marshall Cavendish
Benchmark

New York

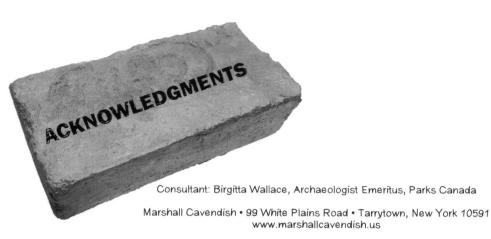

ACKNOWLEDGMENTS

Consultant: Birgitta Wallace, Archaeologist Emeritus, Parks Canada

Marshall Cavendish • 99 White Plains Road • Tarrytown, New York 10591
www.marshallcavendish.us

Text, maps, and illustrations copyright © 2010 by Marshall Cavendish Corporation
All rights reserved. No part of this book may be reproduced or utilized in any form or by
any means electronic or mechanical including photocopying, recording, or by any information
storage and retrieval system, without permission from the copyright holders.

Library of Congress Cataloging–in–Publication Data

Huey, Lois Miner.
American archaeology uncovers the Vikings / by Lois Miner Huey.
p. cm. — (American archaeology)
Includes bibliographical references and index.
ISBN 978–0–7614–4270–7
1. Vikings — North America — Juvenile literature. 2. America — Discovery and
exploration — Norsen — Juvenile literature. 3. Newfoundland and
Labradorn — Antiquitiesn — Juvenile literature. 4. North American — Discovery and
explorationn — Norsen — Juvenile literature. I. Title.
E105.H898 2010
948'.02––dc22

2008050266

Front cover: Top: Students conduct a dig at a science camp sponsored by the University of Connecticut.
Artifacts: left, spindle whorl: center, rune stone: right, butternut
Cover photos: AP Images/Bob Child (top); Parks Canada/G. Vandervloogt (bottom, left); iStockphoto/Johnny
Magnusson (bottom, center); Parks Canda/Shane Kelly (bottom, right) brick; Vishnu Mulakala, dirt; Lisa
ThorinbergBack cover: iStock © Alex Nikado

Photo research by: Tracey Engel
Alamy: Mary Evans Picture Library, 24; Performance Image, 35; David Muenker, 43; Arco Images/Hicker, R.,
51. AP Images: Bob Child, 4. New York State Museum, Albany, NY, 12230: 5 (bottom). Beinecke Rare Book
and Manuscript Library, Yale University: 29. Corbis: Bettmann, 9. The Granger Collection, New York: 12–13,
22, 23, 26–27. Getty Images: Emory Kristof/National Geographic, 30, 32–33; David McLain/Aurora, 44–45.
iStockphoto: Johnny Magnusson, 10; Chris Hepburn, 19. 2005 Lynn E. Noel, Licensed under the Creative
Commons, http://creativecommons.org/licenses/by–nc–sa/3.0/: 25. North Wind Picture Archives: 20–21. Parks
Canada: G. Vandervloogt, 40, 46; D. Crawford, 47 (top); D. Brown, 47 (bottom); Shane Kelly, 48. Peter Arnold,
Inc.: Hicker, R., 28. Shutterstock: J. Helgason, 17. Birgitta Wallace: 36. 2; iStock © Kais Tolmats, 3; iStock ©
Eric Isselee, 4; iStock © ObservePhoto, 5; Shutterstock © Najin, 6; iStock © Richard Goerg, iStock © Richard
Cano, 10; Shutterstock © Biuliq, 16; iStock © Norman Chan

Printed in Malaysia
135642

CONTENTS

WHAT IS Historical Archaeology?

Archaeologists dig into the ground to find food bones, building remains, and tools used by people in the past. Historical archaeologists are looking for clues about what happened in America after Europeans arrived.

A group of students at the "Kids Are Scientists, Too" camp conduct an archaeological investigation at the former site of an eighteenth-century home on the University of Connecticut campus at Storrs.

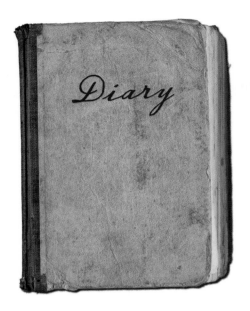

Yes, written documents tell some of the story. Historical archaeologists research documents like maps, diaries, land deeds, and letters to help understand what happened on a site. But those documents do not usually talk about regular people, the ones who did not write letters or diaries. Historical archaeologists are especially interested in learning about the lives of servants, poor farmers, and soldiers who built America.

How do archaeologists do this? By studying people's garbage.

What folks used and threw away tells more about their daily lives than objects kept on shelves out of harm's way. Archaeologists want to study the stuff that did not make it into museums—objects that were broken and discarded after much use. The garbage.

Broken dishes and glassware tell archaeologists what people of the past chose for setting their tables. Studying the bones of people's food, as well as their butchering techniques, provides information about what people ate and how they cooked. When archaeologists measure uncovered house and barn foundations, they find out how people crafted buildings, what size and shape they were, and how they were used. Buttons, straight pins, gun parts, and toys are clues to how people dressed, defended their homes, and spent their leisure time.

How do historical archaeologists know they are collecting information about people who lived in the 1600s rather than people from the 1800s? They use a method called stratigraphy (struh-TIG-ra-fee). Over time, layers of soil called strata build up on a site through natural causes or when people add their own materials. By carefully scraping away the soil with small tools, archaeologists dig down through time. They begin with upper levels of soil, in which they may find nineteenth-century layers. As they work their way down, they reach eighteenth-century layers, seventeenth-century layers, and so on. In some areas, the layers go back as far as Viking times. Prehistoric Native American layers are often found at the deepest level. The scientists dig each layer separately and collect its artifacts. Once the uppermost layer has been removed, the archaeologists have dug through the lives of everyone who lived on that site at a given time.

Based on what they find, archaeologists interpret the artifacts from each time period to understand how people's lives changed. *Change* is a big word in archaeology. How people lived—and how and when that changed—is an important part of the interpretation. As new evidence appears, archaeologists sometimes have to change their interpretations. That makes archaeology really interesting.

Stratigraphy is the key to understanding the past. Sticking a shovel straight down into the ground and pulling up the soil would disturb the stratigraphy, mix up the layers, and mix up the time periods. Archaeologists use shovel testing only to find a site. Then they switch over to small tools and painstakingly remove the layers one by one.

As archaeologists study a site, they carefully draw, map, and photograph building remains. Artifacts are taken back to the lab, where workers wash and store them. Codes are written on each object so that it is clear exactly where the artifact was found. Scientists run tests on charcoal, soil, and remains found inside bottles. Then the archaeologist writes up the results of the research so everyone can know what was learned. Museum displays often follow.

The world which we think of as ours was thought by people in the past to be theirs. Our knowledge of everyday events in the lives of people who lived long ago seems to be washed away by time. By digging in the ground and studying documents, an archaeologist seems to take a voyage to the distant past in a time machine.

Read about archaeology in books and magazines, go to museums, watch programs on television, and maybe visit a local archaeology dig. Someday you, too, might decide to use the tools of archaeology to study the past.

The Vikings In America

The people called Vikings were raiders, explorers, and traders who emerged from the Scandinavian area of northern Europe during a time now known as the Viking Age (about 750 to 1300). Scandinavia has a harsh climate and a short growing season. In this mysterious land of mountains, deep ocean inlets, dense forests, bogs, and meadows, people traveled on the many waterways instead of on land. The Vikings built what were considered the finest ships in Europe.

This illustration shows an eighth–century Viking ship leaving Norway on a trading expedition.

Most of the Norse (or Northmen) thought of themselves as farmers. They had learned to live comfortably with their surroundings. Where they could, Vikings grew crops such as oats, barley, and beans. They herded cattle, goats, and pigs and fished from the sea.

During the long, dark winter months, they often gathered around flickering fires in their longhouses to share stories. Some of these adventure-filled tales told of settlements in Greenland and Iceland—and one in a place called Vinland. The Vikings' stories are called sagas. They were passed down by word of mouth through the generations, and finally they were written down after the end of the Viking Age.

Exciting stories about Viking artifact finds appeal to people all over the world. Unfortunately, most finds are fakes. For example, the Kensington Stone, found near the Red River in Minnesota in 1898, created a sensation.

Writing Runes

Runes were a type of writing that the Norsemen used, mostly to celebrate famous people or deeds. Originally there were twenty-four rune letters, but in the Viking Age, only sixteen were used. People carved runes into stone, metal, and wood. Perhaps because of the sixteen-letter limit, the Norse did not produce long documents or books, only brief descriptions of what they wished to remember. Runes can still be read today.

No authentic rune stones have been found in North America, but as many as three thousand have been found in Sweden. One of the earliest stones, (965 CE) discovered in Denmark, says, "Harold had this stone erected in memory of Gorm his father and Thyra his mother—that Harold who won all Denmark and Norway and made the Danes Christians."

Rune stone in Karlievi, the island of Oland, Sweden. Erected around 1000 CE, the stone commemorates a Danish chief who was buried there.

The runes (writing) on it tell of a Viking voyage from a place called Vinland (pronounced "Vine-land" but meaning "Wine-land") to the heart of North America, where the explorers faced attacks by Native Americans. Although the Kensington Stone proved to be a fake, many people still believe it is a true Viking find, and it still resides in a museum.

In the 1830s, some Americans believed that a round tower in Newport, Rhode Island, was a Viking monument. Today we know it is a windmill built in the 1600s. Stone carvings in Oklahoma, rune stones from Maine, and relics from Ontario, Canada, all turned out to be false traces of the Vikings.

In all, more than fifty sites, one hundred inscriptions, and seventy-five artifacts (swords, spears, and other objects) have been proclaimed to belong to the Vikings—and then identified as fakes. So where *can* traces of Vikings be found?

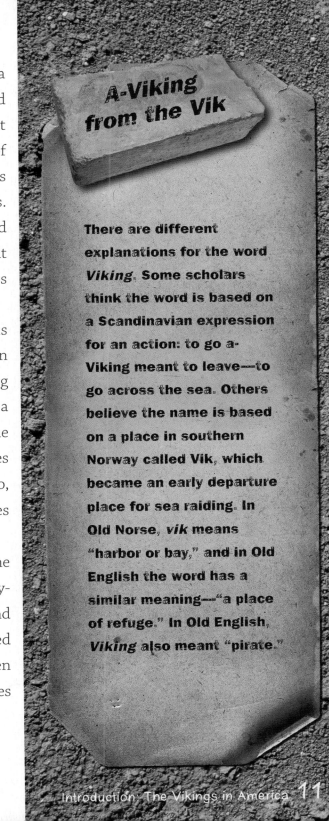

A-Viking from the Vik

There are different explanations for the word *Viking*. Some scholars think the word is based on a Scandinavian expression for an action: to go a-Viking meant to leave—to go across the sea. Others believe the name is based on a place in southern Norway called Vik, which became an early departure place for sea raiding. In Old Norse, *vik* means "harbor or bay," and in Old English the word has a similar meaning—"a place of refuge." In Old English, *Viking* also meant "pirate."

One
The Viking Age

By the end of the eighth century, a period of global warming had melted ice and opened the seas. Now crops could be grown much farther north than before. During this period, called the Medieval Warm Period (ca. 750–1300), the Norse left their homeland in their swift, sleek boats to invade and explore other lands.

This colored engraving depicts a Norse raid under King Olav I of Norway around 994 CE.

Global Warming, Medieval Style

In northern Europe between 750 and 1300, a period of warm, stable weather occurred. These were some of the warmest five centuries since the last ice age. The climate change also affected Greenland, Iceland, and North America. In the north, there was less ice than before (or after), which made conditions very favorable for voyages across the North Sea. During these five centuries of milder weather, farmers produced abundant food with few crop failures. Populations expanded, and great churches were built.

After 1200, the weather began turning colder, and what is called the Little Ice Age lasted until almost 1850. Available farmland shrank, rivers froze, the northern ice pack increased, and life became more difficult. Since 1850, there has been a warming period again. This may be due to natural cycles or to the amount of carbon that industries and automobiles have put into the air—or both.

Scandinavia, with its small amount of good farming and grazing land, had become crowded. The countries of Norway, Sweden, and Denmark were beginning to form. Power struggles associated with this process forced some leaders out. Many of these chieftains took to the sea to seek profit and glory. They searched for new kinds of food, furs, luxury items, and captives to turn into slaves. These raiders were called Vikings. The Norsemen who stayed at home were not called Vikings.

The Viking raiders spread terror and destruction as they swept over the known world. Vikings from present-day Sweden concentrated mostly on the Baltic Sea region and on the shores of Russian rivers, where they collected furs and slaves. Meanwhile, the Danes turned eastward across Europe and south along the coast of Europe into Holland and across the channel to England. The Norwegians concentrated their energies to the north and west. They sailed to

Scotland and the islands around Great Britain, then westward to Iceland, Greenland, and, finally, Vinland. Other Norwegians raided the coast of France and established a country called Normandy.

Most of these raids happened in waves. They were attempts to gain trade goods, land, and slaves. By the late 800s, however, large armies began to swoop out from Scandinavia. For example, in 991, ninety-three ships with partly Swedish crews sailed under the direction of a Norwegian king. These armies extorted large amounts of silver and other plunder, especially from England, where the Vikings ruled much of the country for a while. More than once, the Vikings attacked Paris, Rome, and even Constantinople (today's city of Istanbul) in Turkey. Success in these raids gave those who participated not only profit, but also honor. The Vikings became heroes to the Norse at home.

This map shows the routes of the Viking raids through Europe to North America from 793 to 1000 C.E.

A Bit about Viking Ships

Before the Vikings adopted Christianity, they often buried their dead in boats topped with mounds of soil. The high clay content in the soil helped preserve some of the wood. More often, however, archaeologists find just the iron nails and rivets, which sometimes outline the shape and lines of the ship. Archaeologists also have excavated ships that the Vikings deliberately sank in order to block harbors from possible enemies.

The Vikings built ships by overlapping oak planks and fastening them with iron rivets. This formed a watertight shell. Builders then stabilized and stiffened the shell by inserting ribs inside it. This process was different from the later Mediterranean style, in which builders first erected the ribs, keel (bottom), and stern and then covered them with planks.

Vikings made the boat's keel out of an oak tree with a trunk about 60 feet (18 meters) long. More tree trunks, each about 16.5 feet (5 m) long, were cut in half and then cut in half again to produce wedge-shaped planks for the sides of the ship. In the Viking Age, builders improved on their rowers' speed by introducing a huge woolen sail reinforced with ribbons. Sailors still rowed the ships during times of calm winds and to maneuver into landing spots. Also vital to Viking boats was the side rudder, or rowing oar, mounted near the stern on the right side—in a Scandinavian language *styrbord* or in English *starboard*.

Modern reproductions of Viking ships reveal much about the original vessels. Viking ships were remarkably fast and must have overwhelmed the *skin boats* of the Irish, French, and Englishmen. Foreigners so respected and dreaded the Viking ships—used mostly as troop transports rather than as weapons—that we have no record of them sailing north to plunder Viking homelands.

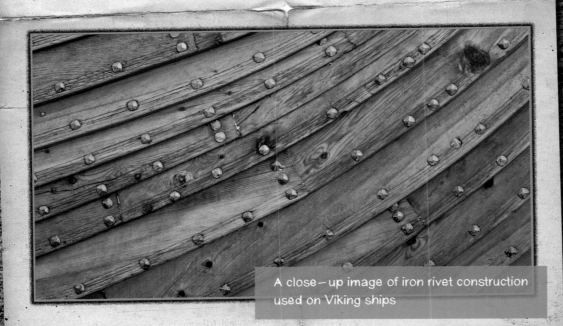

A close—up image of iron rivet construction used on Viking ships

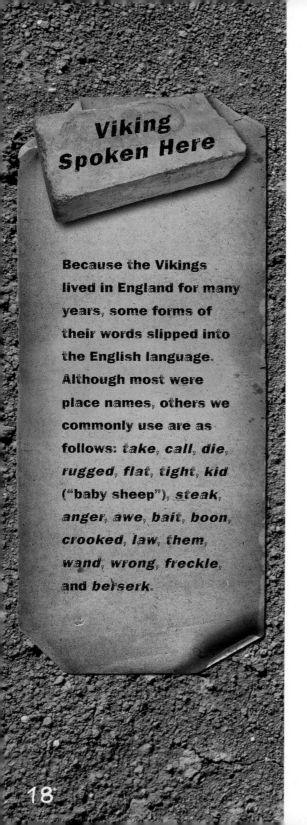

Viking Spoken Here

Because the Vikings lived in England for many years, some forms of their words slipped into the English language. Although most were place names, others we commonly use are as follows: *take, call, die, rugged, flat, tight, kid* ("baby sheep"), *steak, anger, awe, bait, boon, crooked, law, them, wand, wrong, freckle,* and *berserk.*

Eventually the Viking raiders returned to settle some of the lands they had invaded. They established Dublin in Ireland, York in northern England, and other cities around Europe. In eastern Europe, the Vikings were called Rus, and those who settled there ruled much of the territory that today is called Russia. The Vikings also settled in Iceland and Greenland. From there, they sailed west to Vinland.

Entire Viking families set up villages, fishing industries, farms, and churches in lands that they had once attacked. Although these settlers were no longer the invaders called Vikings, that term has become commonly accepted to apply to them.

The Viking Age gradually ended as the weather became colder and wetter again. Settlements in northern areas such as Greenland and Iceland grew smaller and smaller. Stories of the raiders' exploits remain, including the Vinland sagas. But until the archaeologists found it, no one remembered where Vinland was.

"London Bridge Is Falling Down"

London Bridge as it looks today. There has been a bridge over the Thames River at or near this site since Roman times.

In 1014, a Viking king and his companions tied ropes and cables to the supporting beams of the wooden bridge in London. As the Vikings strained to row their boats away, the bridge fell down. In the sagas, this was written, "London Bridge is Broken down! Gold is won and bright renown!" It is easy to see how this rhyme was changed and put to music. It is a popular ditty and child's game to this day.

Two
Viking Sagas

The Vinland Sagas contain two similar yet different stories of a land settled by Vikings sailing west from Greenland and Iceland. The sagas differ because the stories were told and retold before being written down. They must be used with care, but the sagas are a form of historical record.

A bard reciting stories and heroic legends to Viking settlers. Vikings are often shown wearing helmets with wings or horns, but archaeologists never have found ones like that.

According to the sagas, famous Viking leader Erik the Red was banished from Norway and settled in Iceland. Erik then left Iceland and discovered a large island with green meadows and safe harbors. Naming this new land Greenland, Erik sailed back to Iceland and persuaded many inhabitants there to resettle in Greenland.

Erik the Red's son, Leif Eriksson (sometimes called Leif the Lucky), decided to take followers even farther west. While exploring a new land that Leif named Vinland, they settled in one spot but sent out small groups to explore the surrounding area. When the groups returned to Greenland, they carried a cargo of furs, lumber, and grapes—hence the name Wine-land.

Leif's brother, his sister Freydis, and other members of his family also made trips to Vinland. A woman named Gudrid, Leif's sister-in-law, had remarried after the death of Leif's brother. She accompanied her new husband to Vinland. There she gave birth to a son and named him Snorri, a common Scandinavian name. Snorri may have been the first European child born in

A nineteenth-century engraving shows Leif Eriksson and his crew at sea.

The Strange Skraelings

The Skraelings were ancestors of the Micmac or Malisee tribes who occupied the Vinland area. *Skraelings* is a mysterious Norse word whose meaning is unknown. We do know that it was not a flattering term. The Vikings described the people they met in North America as short with dark, tangled hair. Their eyes were large and their cheekbones broad. These people traveled in skin boats and were fascinated with the light-skinned, blond Vikings. Trade between the Vikings and the Skraelings began. The natives were interested especially in obtaining pieces of red cloth in exchange for furs.

One trading session was going well when a loudly bellowing Viking bull ran out of the forest. The Skraelings ran to their boats and rowed off. When they returned, they attacked the Vikings, who defended themselves but then decided to leave. This contact probably took place in what today is New Brunswick, Canada. At another battle recounted in the sagas, Erik the Red's pregnant daughter, Freydis, who apparently had inherited his fiery temper, grabbed the sword of a dead Viking, slapped it across her breast, and threatened the attackers. The Skraelings ran back to their boats and rowed away.

North America. Eventually, because of problems with local inhabitants whom the Vikings called Skraelings, the Europeans left their settlement and returned to Greenland.

In spite of differences between the two Vinland sagas, it seems clear that around the year 1000, people from Greenland and Iceland went on several voyages to North America. They built a settlement so they could spend winters there while exploring the region. Coming into contact with the people they called Skraelings, they traded with them and eventually fought them.

Without proof, however, the sagas are just good stories. Many questions remain. Were the sagas true? Did the Vikings really discover America? If so, where was Vinland?

According to the sagas, Snorri and his parents left Vinland when he was three years old. After a year in Norway, they returned to their estate in Iceland. After her husband's death and her son's marriage, Gudrid, Snorri's mother, continued her travels. She made a pilgrimage to Rome, mostly by foot,

This charming but inaccurate drawing of the Vinland settlement ("Leif's Booths") is an example of how archaeology revealed what the dwellings actually looked like.

thus becoming one of the best-traveled women in medieval times. While she was gone, Snorri built a church in her honor, something she had promised to do upon her return.

Pleased by her son's gesture, Gudrid retired to life as a nun. Snorri ran the estate for the rest of his life. A grandson and a great grandson of Snorri's became important bishops in Iceland's Christian Church. One of Snorri's descendants built a statue in Iceland. The statue shows Gudrid standing in a Viking boat and holding young Snorri on her shoulder. Both figures are facing toward Newfoundland.

The Gudrid and Snorri statue in Iceland

Digging at Snorri's Farm in Iceland

In 2001, by using machines that can sense objects under the ground, archaeologists found what some believe is the site of Snorri's farm. The house was buried under what is now a hay field. About 95 feet (29m) long, the house had three rooms and well-preserved walls. The floor consisted of tramped clay and peat ash. Wooden benches were raised on either side of the narrow floor. The large amount of slag at the site suggests the occupants may have been producing iron from a nearby bog, just as the archaeologists discovered they had done in Vinland, elsewhere in Iceland, and in Greenland.

Three
Who "Discovered" America?

Who actually "discovered" America is a matter of debate. Although Native Americans were the original inhabitants of North America, few historians give them credit for its discovery. Instead many scholars credit Italian explorer Christopher Columbus, who blundered into the West Indies in 1492, as being the first European "discoverer."

This 1895 drawing is titled "Landing of the Norsemen in North America." Note the winged horns on the helmet of the man on the left—archaeologists have found no evidence of these.

Archaeological research has shown that the Vikings built homes in North America five hundred years before Columbus arrived. The Vikings clearly played a role in "discovering" the New World.

Unfortunately, the Vikings left no maps of their settlement. Although many people suspected Vinland was somewhere in the New World, no one knew where. Few people trusted the sagas since they were not written down until many years after the Vinland settlement supposedly took place.

A Norwegian explorer, Helge Ingstad, and his archaeologist wife, Anne, were convinced that Vinland was in North America. They spent much energy, money, and two years exploring the east coast of the continent by boat as they followed clues provided by the sagas and interviewed local inhabitants. In 1960, a farmer named George Decker led Helge to a series of bumps and

ANNE STINE OG
HELGE INGSTAD

De oppdaget vikingenes Amerika

A bronze memorial sculpture of Anne Stine and Helge Ingstad stands in Newfoundland, Canada.

In 1965, Yale University announced the discovery of a map showing the location of Vinland. The reaction was enormous. Scholars rushed to examine it, and scientists were anxious to establish its authenticity. No one has ever claimed that the Vikings themselves drew the map, but it appeared to have been drawn in the early 1400s. Strangely, many of the map's features were unknown during that century, and its black ink is falling off—something that does not occur on early maps. Scientific study of the ink revealed that it contained commercial elements not available before modern times. The Vinland map was another fake.

The Vinland Map

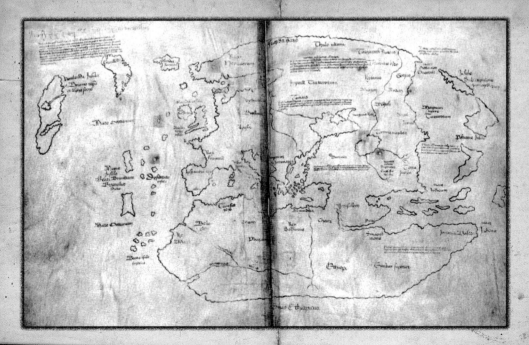

This is an aerial view of the excavation site at L' Anse aux Meadows.

ridges on the northern tip of Newfoundland, an island located just off Canada's eastern coast. Intrigued by what they saw, the Ingstads returned in July 1961 to investigate these features. They were near a small fishing village called L' Anse aux Meadows (pronounced by locals as "Lancy Meadows"). The Ingstads recruited local villagers to help uncover the site. They spent seven summers excavating there.

When they began work, the Ingstads weren't sure if they had found a Viking site. Perhaps it was an Inuit settlement, a Native American village, or a fishermen's town. But the bumps and ridges at the site resembled those seen at Viking sites in Greenland and Iceland. They hoped they had located Vinland.

After uncovering some structures and finding Viking artifacts, they announced that they had found a Viking site. Few people believed them. Why?

No authenticated artifacts or Viking sites in the New World had been found until the Ingstads announced theirs. In addition, the name *Vinland* in Old Norse means "Land of Grapes." But grapes don't grow in Newfoundland, not even during the Medieval Warming Period. So how could this be Wine-land?

The sagas talk about a winter in Vinland when there was no snow. Some have interpreted "no snow" to mean "not as much as we are used to." However, archaeologist Birgitta Linderoth Wallace points out that there was little to no snow in Newfoundland in the winter of 1998 and 1999, "so winters are likely to have been snow-free in the warmer climate of the eleventh century."

Could this site be Vinland? It was a mystery. Archaeologists needed to find the answer through excavation and interpretation of what they had found.

Four
The L' Anse aux Meadows Site

The Ingstads worked at L' Anse aux Meadows between 1961 and 1968. From 1973 to 1976, archaeologists from the national Canadian park service, Parks Canada, excavated more. They concentrated their work in the peat bog area downhill from the buildings that the Ingstads had found.

Archaeologists were photographed excavating the L' Anse aux Meadows site in 1964

The site, still called L' Anse aux Meadows, is located on a dry, windswept terrace of raised land. It is only about 300 feet (90 m) long, less than the length of a football or soccer field, and is located inland from the Atlantic Ocean. *L' Anse* is a French term for a bay or cove, while *aux* means "of." The word *Meadows* is a corruption of the French word *Meduses* for the mythical Greek woman Medea. Scientific tests on plant remains found at the site show that when the Vikings arrived, the land mostly was covered with trees, brush, and bogs still there today. A small brook called Black Duck Brook runs through the site to the sea.

The archaeological excavations showed that when the Vikings settled at L' Anse aux Meadows, there were no Skraelings living there. However, the natives had been there two hundred years earlier, and there was some evidence that Dorset Inuit also had been present earlier. Indian tribes did occupy the site later, in the thirteenth century, but not in the eleventh and twelfth centuries when the Vikings arrived.

In the ridges, the Ingstads uncovered the walls of eight houses, named simply Houses A through J (some letters identify specific rooms inside the buildings). Seven of these houses were arranged into three separate complexes lined up north-south across the terrace and built about 100 feet (30 m) apart. A complex consisted of a great hall with three interior rooms and a small, one-room hut close by.

The A-B-C complex farthest south also had a third, much larger house, called B. The dwellings were built like those in Iceland, and the arrangement inside indicates they were erected in the eleventh century, which is when the sagas say Vikings explored North America. The eighth building, J, was built on the other side of the brook, close to the shore of Black Duck Creek.

An unusual characteristic of L' Anse aux Meadows was the lack of barns and animal pens found on farms. Cows, goats, and sheep must have been pastured in the open. The lack of outbuildings and the arrangement of the structures indicate that L' Anse aux Meadows was not a colony but a base where a large group of people, perhaps three ship crews, stayed during the winter months. It took two weeks to a month to sail to Greenland. Therefore, in order to carry out explorations in the L' Anse aux Meadows area, Vikings needed to stay over the winter so they could explore for a much longer time in spring and fall.

Making Iron—A First in North America

The discovery and excavation of Hut J proved to be of great importance for understanding what was happening in the three complexes. In Hut J, located on the bank of Black Duck Creek,

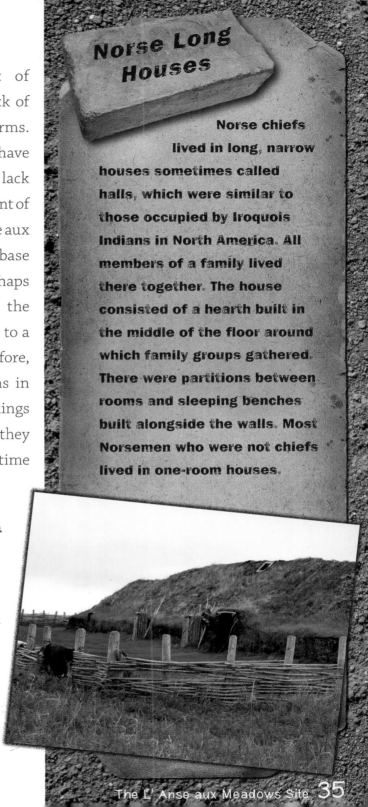

Norse Long Houses

Norse chiefs lived in long, narrow houses sometimes called halls, which were similar to those occupied by Iroquois Indians in North America. All members of a family lived there together. The house consisted of a hearth built in the middle of the floor around which family groups gathered. There were partitions between rooms and sleeping benches built alongside the walls. Most Norsemen who were not chiefs lived in one-room houses.

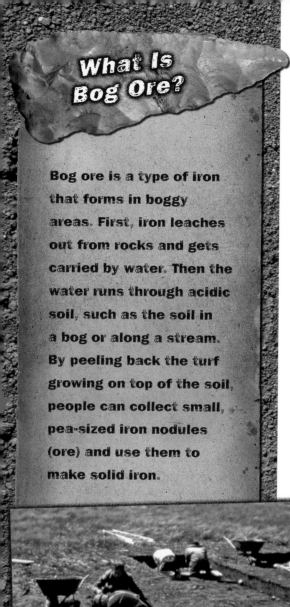

What Is Bog Ore?

Bog ore is a type of iron that forms in boggy areas. First, iron leaches out from rocks and gets carried by water. Then the water runs through acidic soil, such as the soil in a bog or along a stream. By peeling back the turf growing on top of the soil, people can collect small, pea-sized iron nodules (ore) and use them to make solid iron.

Archaeologists uncover a layer of bog ore at L' Anse aux Meadows.

archaeologists found evidence of the first known manufacturing of iron in North America.

The Vikings first dug into the creek bank and set posts and sod to form the back and two sides of the hut. The side toward the brook was left open. A small stone frame covered with clay was set over a shallow pit in the ground. This formed a furnace. Workers collected bog ore from the surrounding bogs. To make the bog ore usable, it first was roasted on a bed of fresh wood so that its water content boiled off. The ore that was left was packed into the furnace between layers of charcoal. In another nearby pit, the Vikings burned wood to produce charcoal.

Because charcoal burns at a much higher temperature than wood, it works well for smelting iron. Tests show that the furnace at L' Anse aux Meadows reached a temperature of 2,282 degrees Fahrenheit (1,250 degrees Celsius), plenty hot enough to turn the iron into liquid. The melted iron ran down into the bottom of the pit. When cooled, it looked like a sponge.

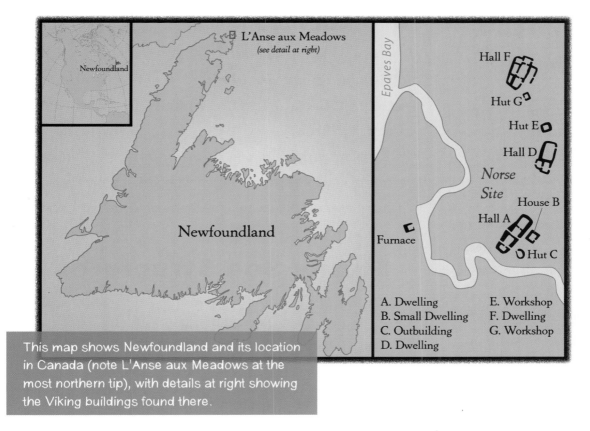

Hall F

Hut G

Hut E

Hall D

Norse Site

House B

Hall A

Hut C

Furnace

Epaves Bay

L' Anse aux Meadows
(see detail at right)

Newfoundland

Newfoundland

A. Dwelling
B. Small Dwelling
C. Outbuilding
D. Dwelling

E. Workshop
F. Dwelling
G. Workshop

This map shows Newfoundland and its location in Canada (note L'Anse aux Meadows at the most northern tip), with details at right showing the Viking buildings found there.

The Vikings removed the iron sponge, reheated it, and hammered it at a high temperature to remove impurities. Then it was ready for the forge, where blacksmiths turned it into boat nails.

Tests done on the cut and discarded nails at the site revealed that the nails were made elsewhere. Pulled from boats, they had been replaced by new ones manufactured at L' Anse aux Meadows. Tests on the one whole nail found showed that it was made at L' Anse aux Meadows. It probably had been dropped and lost before it could be used.

Probably slaves collected bog ore and dug the pit where charcoal was made. Both tasks must have been done during good weather. Thus, most of the slaves probably stayed at the settlement during summer and early fall.

The smelting of iron in the furnace, however, probably happened during chilly weather because a building had been erected above the furnace to protect it. Expert craftsmen probably did the smelting.

Eventually someone tore down the stone furnace and threw it down the bank along with some waste called slag. Hundreds of years later, the archaeologists came across it.

Sturdy Sod Structures

The longhouse buildings found at L' Anse aux Meadows were similar to those on Viking sites in Iceland. They were intended to be permanent structures. Their thick walls were made of sod supported on the inside by lines of posts. The centers of the walls were filled with gravel and sand. Roofs had wooden frames covered with more sod.

Parks Canada archaeologist Birgitta Wallace estimates it would have taken about 35,000 cubic feet (990 cubic meters) of sod to construct each of the halls and eighty-six large trees for support posts, beams, and branches woven between the rafters to form the roof frame. The Vikings needed even more wood for the paneled walls inside the houses and the wooden platforms built along the sidewalls. Each of these structures, then, required a great deal of labor. Longhouses certainly were not just summer shelters.

Life in Leif's Hall

The northern hall, complex F–G, was the largest and the most lived in, as more artifacts were found there than in other structures. The leader of the L' Anse aux Meadows expedition, Leif the Lucky, probably was the first to live there with his crew.

Six rooms were found inside this complex. A kitchen was in an annex on the west side. It was 11 feet (3 m) by 14 feet (4 m) in size, large enough to hold several people. It probably was used for butchering animals and brewing beer. The kitchen's oven was constructed of stones set on edge, over which there would have been a covering of smaller stones. The occupants probably also used the oven to create steam for a sauna. The Norse often sat in hot, steamed-up rooms to relax, to talk, and to clean themselves. Next door was a storage room, most likely for food supplies, utensils, and items to be shipped back home.

Boat repair occurred in a lean-to attached to the east side of Hall F. Of the more than eighty nail fragments found on the site, over half were located around this lean-to. The nails had been snipped off and thrown away. At other Viking sites, these kinds of nails are found only in places where boat and ship repair was ongoing. Nails exposed to salt water need frequent replacement. X-rays of the nails revealed that they had been cut and their washers split with a chisel so they could be pulled easily from boat planks.

Other artifacts found in the F–G complex included round, soft rocks whose centers had been pecked out to create a hollow. These could have been used as lamps, in which a wick burning in oil would have created a flickering light. Viking stone lamps are a frequent find on Viking sites. The discovery of a bone needle and a soapstone spindle whorl used for weaving indicated that women were present. The spindle whorl, most likely carved from a broken Norse

Artifacts found include a spindle whorl (top left), a bone pin (top right), and a bone needle (bottom).

soapstone pot, was found at the site. One side of the spindle whorl was flat and crusted with a burned substance.

Stone tools called strike-a-lights were used for starting fires. They were an important find at L' Anse aux Meadows. The type of jasper stone used to make these tools came from Greenland. In the other two halls archaeologists found strike-a-lights made from a type of jasper found in Iceland. This suggested that there were three different groups from three different ships living on the site—one from Greenland living in the F-G complex and the others from Iceland in the other two complexes.

Boat Crew's Quarters

The middle hall complex, D–E, was smaller than the others and contained no private chambers. A large open area in Longhouse D would have held about twenty people. The inhabitants all slept, ate, and talked in one large room. Judging by the strike-a-lights and large storage room, this area may have been the quarters for an Iceland boat crew.

One room in the hall was a carpenter's shop with an opening toward the peat bog. Fragments of large broken objects, including parts of boats, were discarded here after the carpenter made replacements. Hundreds of pieces of wood debris also were found outside the door of Building E. Similar to weaving huts found in Iceland, Building E had a stone oven and nineteen stones probably used as loom weights inside. Women probably used this building and Hall D for weaving.

A birch bark cylinder (found in the bog outside Hall D) and birch bark rolls (found in the bog outside Building E) could have been used for net fishing. Filled with stone, they would have weighed the nets down so they would not float away. Stones found in a corner of Building E on its bog side could have been the sinkers used in these containers.

Chieftain's Complex

The southernmost complex of buildings was the second largest. It held about thirty-five people—another group from Iceland. Because this complex also had separate rooms, a chieftain probably lived there.

Archaeologists found artifacts relating to daily life inside and around the halls. In Hall A, for example, they discovered wood cut for fires, hearth stones that had been heated, a bronze pin used to fasten a cloak, iron nails and rivets, cooked food bones, a birch bark container, jasper strike-a-lights, a stone pounder, tar used for repairs, and a grinding stone.

A workshop was located in the center of Hall A. Pieces of waste from a blacksmith's shop suggest that smithing happened there. As in Iceland, people used the workshop for heating iron and pounding it into objects, most likely nails.

This complex also had a small house, B. The person in charge of iron manufacturing might have lived there, as evidenced by roasted bog ore found inside.

A round hut, C, although poorly built, had a fireplace inside. Slaves most likely lived there. Vikings took slaves to Vinland to cut the sod and wood for buildings and to help the craftsmen repair boats.

A Viking approaching one of the halls would walk in through doors located in the sidewalls, away from ocean winds. He or she could choose from two entrances, one near the southeast corner and one in the center. The weavers entered

Building B, the largest of the huts, through a door near its southeastern corner.

Vikings living in each complex gathered around the hearth in the largest room, and many slept on the side platforms. Chieftains and their wives slept in the smaller private rooms. During the summer months, the buildings were mostly empty, as many of the men left in their boats to explore areas to the south and to gather items such as grapes, wood for lumber, and other food not found in Newfoundland, Greenland, or Iceland. The slaves, women, and some men stayed at L' Anse aux Meadows to hunt, fish, and gather plants to build up a food supply for the cold months. Nets were spread close to shore to catch fish before the bay froze over. The fish were dried on racks and stored away.

Cooking occurred inside the big hall of each complex on the 8-foot-long (2.4-meter-long) central hearth built directly on the floor. An open fire, a cooking pit, and a pit where glowing embers could be kept alive for use in the morning were vital for cooking, light, and warmth.

The soil at the L' Anse aux Meadows site is very acidic, so food bones decay rapidly there. This makes it difficult for archaeologists to figure out exactly what the Vikings ate. Most of the bone they found came from seals, whales, and codfish. Seals and whales were hunted during the winter months, and fish was netted and dried during the summer. However, many of the bones found had been cooked until they turned white. Cooked white bone comes from making stews, which appeared to be the preferred daily food. The Vikings must have brought cattle, sheep, and goats with them to the site in order to make milk, butter, cheese, and *skyr*, a favorite kind of yogurt.

During winter, between November and June, the women continued their household chores. The men repaired their boats—their vital link to home. Their work done, they gathered around the warm fires, ate dried fish, told stories, and celebrated Christmas. The Vikings loved walnuts, which were expensive treats imported to Greenland from continental Europe. Only chieftains could afford them. The settlers must have been excited when they found butternuts, a North American variety of the walnut family, growing wild. They apparently collected the butternuts from areas farther south.

Happenings in the Huts

Seven to fourteen people could have lived in the small huts and annexes in the complexes. The sod walls of these workshops had roofs supported by posts along the sides. Fires were located not in the center but directly on the floor next to a wall. A large, upright stone slab protected the wall from the flames. The unique fire location opened up the small area inside for work and living space.

This interior view of a building at the site shows the sod walls and timber posts supporting the roof.

Five

What Archaeologists Found Out

When the inhabitants of L' Anse aux Meadows left the site, they took tools and equipment with them. The only artifacts left behind were either lost or left over from mending ships, extracting iron from bog ore, and making nails from the iron.

A view of the reconstructed village at L'Anse aux Meadows

The artifacts found on the site, although few, are definitely Viking. Some were found on the floors of the halls; others sat in deposits of ash, charcoal, food bones, and broken items swept out a door. Many had been thrown into bogs.

One exciting find was a ringed bronze pin, a telltale Viking object. It had a distinct West Norse design common to the tenth and early eleventh centuries. Both male and female Vikings used these pins to fasten cloaks; thirteen of them have been found on Iceland sites. A glass bead and women's tools such as a broken bone knitting needle, stone spindle whorls, and a small whetstone used to sharpen needles, scissors, and small knives were left behind. Stone lamps like one found at the site are common Viking artifacts. One mysterious object is a small brass loop. It had been gilded with gold. Was this once attached to a piece of expensive jewelry? Such a priceless object indicates that some wealthy people lived at the site.

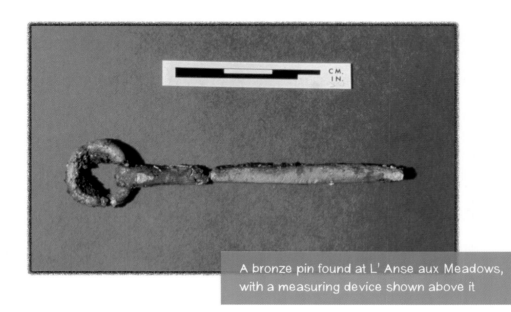

A bronze pin found at L' Anse aux Meadows, with a measuring device shown above it

Wooden objects found in the wet areas—where they were well preserved—include a notched wooden bow fragment, a spruce plank that might have come from a tent pole, a barrel top, spruce rope used to fasten barrel hoops, and a small birch bark container sewn with thinner spruce rope.

A wood plank found at L' Anse aux Meadows

All these objects are common to Viking sites of the late tenth and eleventh centuries. They all show signs of having been formed by iron tools, which local Indian tribes did not have. These, then, were the work of Europeans.

Some of the most important objects discovered at the site were the butternuts. The archaeologists found the nuts in the bogs along with a butternut burl (growth on a tree) that had been cut with a metal tool. Butternut trees do not grow in Newfoundland, not even during the Medieval Warming Period. They do grow in the Saint Lawrence River valley and in New Brunswick, both south of Newfoundland, where wild grapes also are found. The presence of butternuts at the

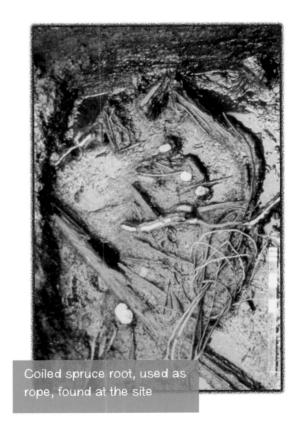

Coiled spruce root, used as rope, found at the site

A butternut found at the site

site shows that the people who lived at L' Anse aux Meadows had traveled south to other parts of North America and had picked up objects to bring back.

Vinland, then, is not the name of the L' Anse aux Meadows settlement but of the entire area in North America explored by the Vikings. The site on northern Newfoundland was a base for exploring farther south, to at least New Brunswick and perhaps farther.

The sagas also say that the Viking explorers found large meadows and sheltered areas for their boats to the south. (They also found many Skraelings who didn't take kindly to the newcomers.) Therefore, the name *Vinland*, Birgitta Wallace is convinced, refers to "all the coasts around the Gulf of Saint Lawrence, and L' Anse aux Meadows was the base from which it was explored, the gateway into Vinland."

The strongest evidence that L' Anse aux Meadows was this Viking base is the presence of activities performed by Europeans: boat repair, iron smelting, nail manufacturing, and Viking-style building construction. These activities were almost identical to those of Vikings in Iceland and Greenland.

Tests run on the artifacts, such as the iron nails, provided strong evidence that they were all made elsewhere. An exception was the one complete nail that tests show was made at the site. More than 140 tests were run on charcoal and wood remains. Some revealed an earlier Native American presence, but half dated to the Viking period. Seven of the tests on wood cut and used by the Vikings resulted in a date of between 950 and 1020—exactly the time the Vikings were supposed to have been there.

In Synch with the Sagas

The excavations, combined with information from the sagas, led archaeologists to reach several conclusions. L' Anse aux Meadows is a Viking site, the only one found thus far in North America and one of the most important sites ever found there. It was built on an exposed piece of land, open to the ocean but a good place to watch for enemies and an easy place for visiting ships to find. Permanent

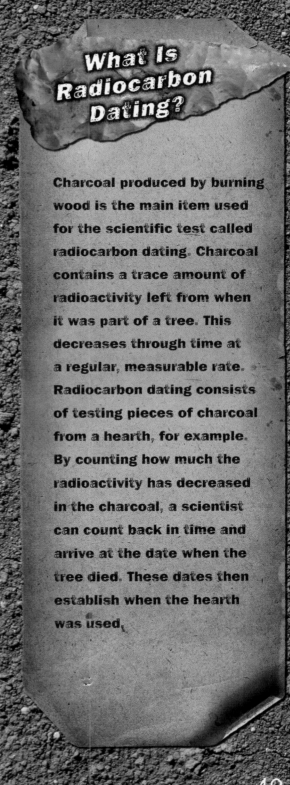

What Is Radiocarbon Dating?

Charcoal produced by burning wood is the main item used for the scientific test called radiocarbon dating. Charcoal contains a trace amount of radioactivity left from when it was part of a tree. This decreases through time at a regular, measurable rate. Radiocarbon dating consists of testing pieces of charcoal from a hearth, for example. By counting how much the radioactivity has decreased in the charcoal, a scientist can count back in time and arrive at the date when the tree died. These dates then establish when the hearth was used.

Is L' Anse aux Meadows the Real Vinland?

Archaeologist Birgitta Wallace answers this way: At the time L' Anse aux Meadows was built, the total population in Greenland numbered only four hundred to five hundred people, including women, children, and elderly people. If just one expedition crew to Newfoundland came from Greenland, that meant ten percent of the people in Greenland had gone to Newfoundland! And these would have been mostly men who were the best workers. The size of L' Anse aux Meadows is consistent with the number of people whom the sagas say came to the site—around one hundred. "It is unthinkable," says Wallace, "that the Greenland Norse would have had sufficient human resources to construct—and, equally important, to operate—a series of posts such as these."

buildings were built to serve three functions: housing, craft activities, and storage. The artifacts found related to iron smelting, blacksmithing, carpentry, and food gathering.

At the base camp of L' Anse aux Meadows, each of the three complexes of buildings had a specific function. After a furnace in Building J pulled iron from bog ore, the blacksmith in complex A-B-C smelted the iron on a forge and turned it into nails. The new iron nails then were used to replace rusted nails in boats hauled to the F-G complex. Carpenters completed further boat repairs in Complex D-E. Expert craftsmen performed these activities but were assisted by others.

Clearing land, digging sod, collecting bog iron, and digging the charcoal pit were the work of slaves who lived in the round hut, Building C.

The choice of this site, construction of the buildings, performance of craft activities, exploration, and gathering of resources were done under the leadership of a strong male figure, just as elsewhere

A museum interpreter reenacts iron smith work at the L' Anse aux Meadows National Historic Site.

in Viking society. Although evidence of male activities here was most common, women were also present. They wove, gathered food, sewed, and cooked.

Birgitta Wallace believes that Leif Eriksson established the first settlement at L' Anse aux Meadows, thus making his personal claim to the land. All those who followed were relatives to whom Eriksson gave permission to use the buildings. In return, they promised him a share of the cargoes they brought back.

The archaeologists found no cemetery, only very small piles of garbage, and few broken artifacts. All of this indicates a short-term occupation of only a few years. The Vikings who came here were part of a wide-ranging movement to explore and to collect resources from all over the world. The furs, grapes, lumber, and nuts found here were not profitable enough. The Vikings probably considered colonizing the rich meadows they found farther south, but problems with Skraelings made them rethink the idea.

The Vikings withdrew from L' Anse aux Meadows and the area they called Vinland to return to Iceland and Greenland, thus leaving the area open for the new European explorers who would follow hundreds of years later.

The L' Anse aux Meadows Site Today

Once excavations were complete, the walls of the Viking site were covered with clean white sand and sod. The ridges and bumps on the landscape still show, however, and each is interpreted for the public with an informational sign.

In an area away from the original site, Parks Canada built a reproduction of a Viking settlement. The interiors of these new longhouses are furnished with copies of items used by the Vikings. Visitors can walk through the hall and ask questions of costumed interpreters who explain their history and duties, just as if they were the original Vikings who lived on the site.

Around 17,000 years ago Peoples from Asia travel by a northern land bridge, or as some believe, also by boat, to settle North America. Columbus later named them Indians.

Around 750 The Medieval Warming Period begins.

870 Vikings settle in Iceland.

886 Vikings rule much of England.

911 Vikings rule over Normandy in northern France.

985 Erik the Red leads settlers to Greenland.

Around 1000 Leif the Lucky discovers and names Vinland.

1014 Vikings under King Olaf pull down London Bridge.

1042 English king Edward the Confessor is crowned.

1066 Viking descendants from Normandy under William the Conqueror invade and conquer England. Some put this date as the end of the Viking Age.

Around 1200 Icelanders begin to record oral sagas passed down since the 800s.

Around 1300 The Medieval Warming Period ends; the Little Ice Age begins.

1492 Europeans under the leadership of Christopher Columbus "rediscover" America.

Around 1850 The Little Ice Age ends; the modern warming period begins.

annex—An addition or wing built onto a main building.

archaeologist—A person who studies life in the past by uncovering and interpreting objects buried over time.

artifact—An object made by people in the past.

banished—Forced out of one's homeland.

bog—A spongy type of wetland.

craftsmen—People skilled at a certain craft, such as a carpenter who works with wood.

descendants—People who are born into a family after a certain individual—i.e., the individual's children, grandchildren, and so on.

excavation—Careful digging up of buried objects to learn about the past.

extort—To force others to give up their money or other treasures.

forge—A place where metal is heated and hammered into shape.

furnace—A place for a very hot fire used by blacksmiths to heat metal so it can be shaped into objects.

ice age—a time period of cold weather and glacial activity on Earth. There have been several ice ages. The last ice age ended around 17,000 years ago.

keel—A long piece of wood that goes from end to end on the bottom of a ship.

lean-to—An addition attached to a main building, sometimes with only three walls.

longhouse—A communal building with a long, narrow shape.

loom—A wooden frame used to weave wool thread into cloth.

Medea—A witch from Greek myths who helped Jason steal the golden fleece but then went crazy and harmed other people. The sea off northern Newfoundland often acted like a crazy person, so it was originally named after her.

peat—A plant covering on top of a bog. Sometimes it is dried and burned as fuel.

raider—A person who unexpectedly attacks other people and their land.

runes—The letters of the Viking alphabet.

Rus (Roos)—Scandinavians, mostly Swedish, who settled in eastern Europe.

sagas—Tales of historical or legendary heroes who explored, raided, and conquered other lands.

settler—A person who leaves his or her own homeland and builds a home in a new place.

skin boats—Boats made by covering a wood frame with sewn animal skins.

slag—The waste left behind when smelting metal.

smelting—Heating ore to remove the metal.

soapstone—A soft rock that can easily be carved into objects.

spindle whorl—A stone or piece of pottery, pierced in the middle, that is placed on a wooden shaft (spindle) to weigh down the wool or cotton while the weaver turns the shaft to make yarn or thread.

terrace—A flat area located upland from water.

Books

Schomp, Virginia. *The Norsemen* (Myths of the World). New York: Marshall Cavendish/Benchmark, 2008.

Weintraub, Aileen. *Vikings Raiders and Explorers*. New York: Scholastic Press, 2005.

Wheatley, Abigail, Struan Reid, John Woodcock, Ian McNee. *The Usborne Introduction to Archaeology: Internet Linked*. Tulsa, OK: EDC Publishing, 2005.

Websites

http://www.canadianmysteries.ca/sites/vinland/home/indexen.html
Learn about the Vikings, Vinland, L' Anse aux Meadows, and other Viking mysteries.

www.mnh.si.edu/vikings
This site covers the Smithsonian exhibit that toured in the year 2000, the anniversary of the Vikings' exploration and settlement in America. The site takes you from room to room of the exhibits and shows Viking artifacts. It is a dramatic presentation, so make sure to have your sound turned on!

www.pbs.org/wgbh/nova/vikings
This site presents a two-hour show that first appeared on the television show *Nova*, plus other videos and information about the Vikings. You can click on one command that will show you what your name looks like in runes.

www.yorkarchaeology.co.uk
Learn about the archaeology of the Viking town York, located in northern England.

FURTHER INFORMATION

Books and Articles

Bolander, Douglas. Interview regarding archaeological work at Snorri's farm in Iceland, Oct. 2007.

dig Magazine. Two issues of this archaeology magazine for kids concentrate on the Vikings. Carus Publishing, in Portsmouth, NH, still carries back issues. Vol. 2 No. 5 and Vol. 8 No. 9, 2000 and 2006.

Includes discussion of the work at L' Anse aux Meadows and other Viking sites around the world.

Fagan, Brian. *The Little Ice Age: How Climate Made History 1300–1850*. New York: Basic Books, 2002.

Fagan's well-known book has a lengthy introduction about the Medieval Warming Period and how it affected historical events around the year 1000.

Fitzhugh, William W. and Elisabeth I. Ward. *The North Atlantic Saga*. Washington, DC: Smithsonian Institution Press, 2000.

The most useful and most recent source used. Includes two extensive articles by archaeologist Birgitta Wallace, discussions of the Vikings in general, archaeology in Iceland and Newfoundland, and translations of the Vinland sagas.

Huey, Paul and Lois Feister-Huey. Notes taken while visiting L' Anse aux Meadows, May 2001.

Ingstad, Anne Stine. *The Discovery of a Norse Settlement in America: Excavations at L' Anse aux Meadows, Newfoundland, 1961–1968*. Translated by Elizabeth Seeberg. New York: Columbia University Press, 1977.

Lewis-Simpson, Shannon, ed. "Vinland Revisited: The Norse World at the Turn of the First Millennium."

Papers given at the Viking Millennium International Symposium, September, 2000.

Historic Sites Association of Newfoundland and Labrador, Inc., St. John's, Newfoundland.

Magnusson, Magnus and Hermann Palsson, eds./translators. *The Vinland Sagas: The Norse Discovery of America.* Baltimore: Penguin Books, 1965.

Editors did an extensive explanatory introduction before presenting English translations of the two Vinland sagas.

Odelberg, Maj, Lena Thålin-Bergman, and Inger Zachrisson. *Viking Ways: On the Viking Age in Sweden.* Stockholm: The Swedish Institute, 1980.

All three authors were archaeologists at the Museum of Natural Antiquities. Booklet contains discussion of various basic topics about Vikings. Purchased at the Nordic Heritage Museum, Seattle, WA.

Orrling, Carin. *Vikings! Traders and Craftsmen.* Exhibit pamphlet from the National Museum of Antiquities, Stockholm, 1984.

Exhibit appeared at the Nordic Heritage Museum, Seattle, WA.

Orser, Charles E., Jr. ed. *Enyclopedia of Historical Archaeology.* London: Routledge, 2003.

Entries on Vikings, St. Augustine, Jamestown, New York, Netherland.

Parks Canada. "Welcome to L' Anse aux Meadows National Historic Site of Canada." 2003 Brochure.

National Parks and National Historic Sites of Canada in Newfoundlandand Labrador, p. 24. Booklet.

Quinn, David B. *North America from Earliest Discovery to First Settlements: The Norse Voyages to 1612.* New York: Harper & Row, 1977.

Seaver, Kirsten A. *The Frozen Echo: Greenland and the Exploration of North America ca A.D. 1000–1500.* Stanford, CA: Stanford University Press, 1996.

Discussions of Norse occupations based on the argument that the Norse stayed in Greenland longer than believed and continued to travel to North America for its resources.

Steinberg, John M. "The Viking Age Long-House at Glaumbaer Skagafjordur, Northern Iceland." *Antiquity,* Vol. 77, No. 295, March 2003.

Article written about excavations of Snorri's house in Iceland.

Wahlgren, Erik. *The Vikings and America.* London: Thames & Hudson Ltd, 2000.

Useful for discussion of sagas but poor on interpretations of L' Anse aux Meadows as he appears to have used only the results of the Ingsteds' work.

Wallace, Birgitta Linderorth. Notes taken by the author while visiting the archeologist of L' Anse aux Meadows at her home in Halifax, May 2003.

Two articles in Fitzhugh's volume, 2000.

"L' Anse aux Meadows, Gateway to Vinland." *Acta Archaeologica*, Vol. 61, Munksgaard, Denmark, 1991.

————Wallace, Birgitta Linderoth. *Westward Vikings: The Saga of L' Anse aux Meadows.* The Historic Sites Association of Newfoundland, Canada and Labrador, St. John's, 2006.

Washburn, Wilcomb E., ed. *Proceedings of the Vinland Map Conference.* Chicago: University of Chicago Press, 1971.

Copies of papers given at a conference at Yale University in 1965.

Websites

www.chronicles-network.com/forum/37987-war-of-the-words.html
A discussion of Old Norse origins of modern English

http://leiferiksson.vanderkrogt.net/files/gudridur_glaumbaer.html
An account of excavations at Snorri's farm in Iceland

www.northvegr.org/lore/norse
Translations and explanatory notes about the Vinland sagas

INDEX

About the Author

Lois Miner Huey is a historical archaeologist working for the State of New York. She has published many articles about history and archaeology in kids' magazines as well as a book biography of the Mohawk Indian woman, Molly Brant. She and her archaeologist husband live near Albany, New York in an old house with four affectionate cats.